D1737373

ORANGUTANS

MARYSA STORM

BLACK
RABBIT
BOOKS

Bolt Jr. is published by Black Rabbit Books
P.O. Box 3263, Mankato, Minnesota, 56002.
www.blackrabbitbooks.com
Copyright © 2020 Black Rabbit Books

Catherine Cates, designer; Omay Ayres, photo researcher

Names: Storm, Marysa, author.
Title: Orangutans / by Marysa Storm.
Description: Mankato, Minnesota : Black Rabbit Books, [2020] | Series: Bolt Jr. Awesome animal lives | Audience: Age 6-8. | Audience: K to Grade 3. | Includes bibliographical references and index.
Identifiers: LCCN 2018054903 (print) | LCCN 2018056492 (ebook) | ISBN 9781623101572 (e-book) | ISBN 9781623101510 (library binding) | ISBN 9781644661017 (paperback)
Subjects: LCSH: Orangutans–Juvenile literature.
Classification: LCC QL737.P94 (ebook) | LCC QL737.P94 S76 2020 (print) | DDC 599.88/3–dc23
LC record available at https://lccn.loc.gov/2018054903

Printed in the United States. 5/19

Image Credits

Alamy: Matjaz Corel, Cover; Dreamstime: Patrimonio Designs Limited, 14; Shutterstock: bimserd, 7; Eric Isselee, 4; FiledIMAGE, 5; Gekko Gallery, 10–11; Grigor Unkovski, 5; GUDKOV ANDREY, 6–7, 10; Kitch Bain, 23; leolintang, 13, 21; Lintang Hakim, 18–19; Sergey Uryadnikov, 16–17, 20–21; Val_Iva, 3; Yatra, 1; Superstock: Michael Nolan / robertharding, 8–9; Suzi Eszterhas / Minden Pictures, 12

Contents

CHAPTER 1

A Day in the Life

An orangutan walks along the forest floor. The animal stops near a log. It grabs a stick and pokes it into the log. Then the orangutan pulls the stick out. It's covered in **honey**. Yum! Time for a treat.

honey: a thick, sweet substance made by bees

orangutan ◄ ······· WEIGHT COMPARISON

73 to 250 pounds
(33 to 113 kilograms)

Smart Animals

Orangutans are smart animals. Their hands and feet grab like human hands. Grabbing lets them use sticks as tools. These animals have long arms. They use them to swing through trees.

▶ gorilla
150 to 500 pounds
(68 to 227 kg)

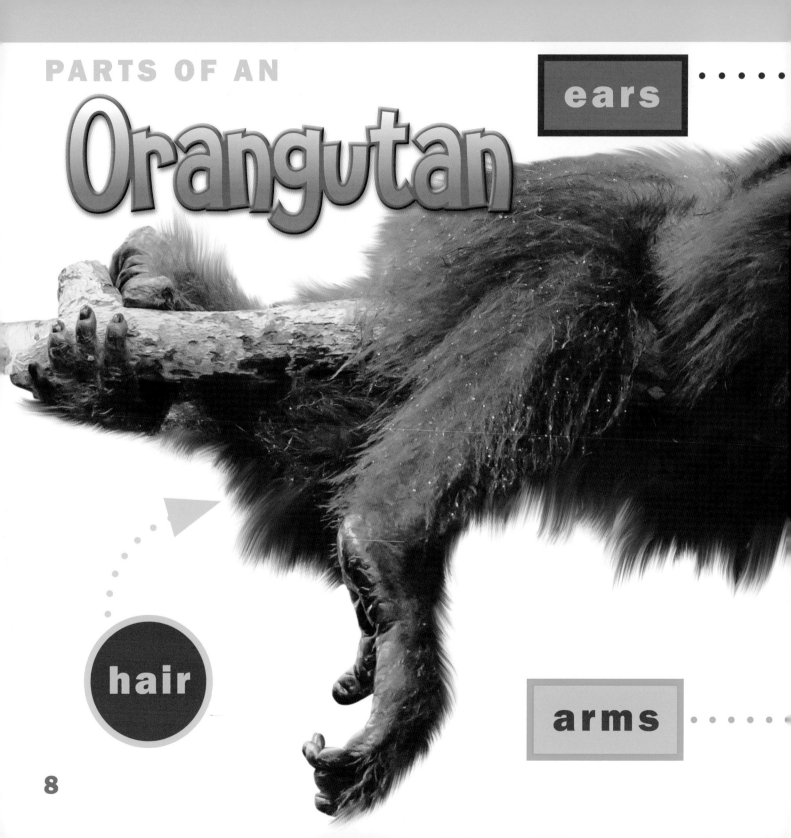

PARTS OF AN

Orangutan

ears

arms

hair

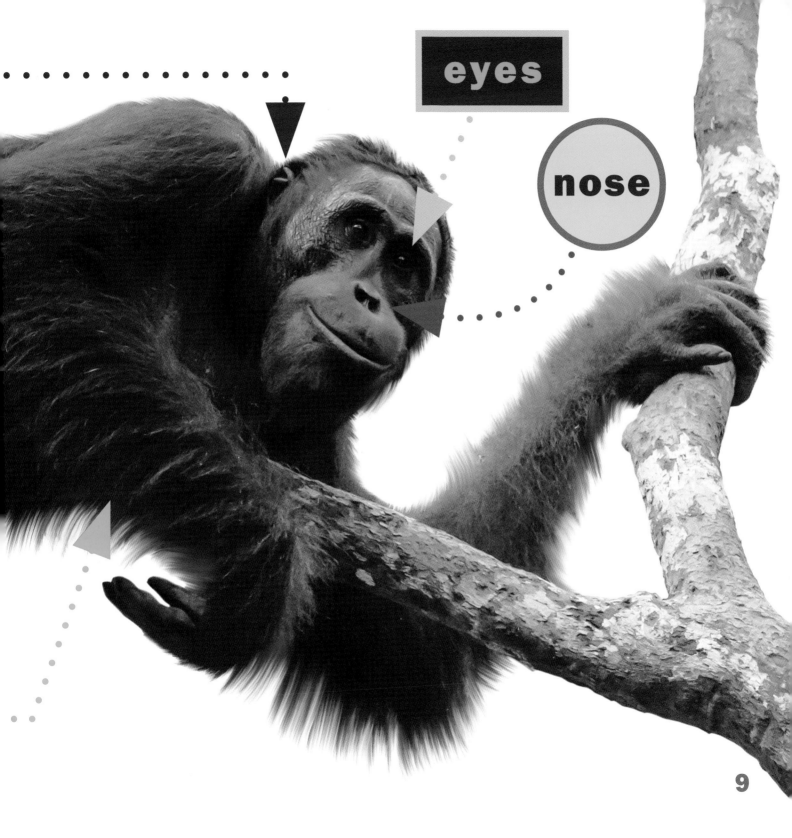

eyes

nose

9

CHAPTER 2

Food and Homes

Orangutans eat plants and animals. They like fruit the best. They also eat leaves and **insects**.

insect: a small animal that has six legs

FACT

Sometimes they eat bird eggs.

Orangutan Homes

These animals live in **rain forests**. They spend most of their time in the trees. They build nests in the branches. They make them from leaves. Every day, they make new nests.

rain forest: a tropical forest that gets a lot of rain and has tall trees

Where Orangutans Live

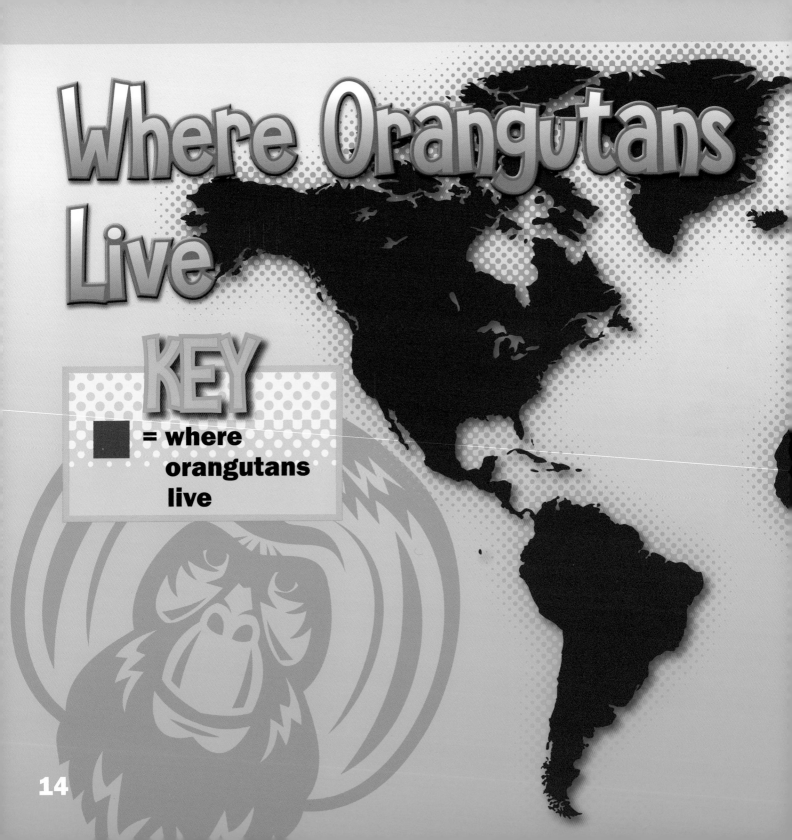

KEY

■ = where orangutans live

CHAPTER 3

Family Life

Orangutans often live alone.
Mothers share their nests with their
babies. Most mothers have one baby
at a time.

FACT

Mothers rarely have twins.

Babies

Babies stay with their mothers for a long time. The mothers protect them from tigers and leopards. They also show the babies what to eat.

When they're about nine, the young leave. They're ready to live alone.

3

Newborn Orangutan's Weight

about 3 pounds (1 kg)

Bonus Facts

Adults have 32 teeth.

They spend **up to 6 hours** looking for food each day.

Wild orangutans live 30 to 40 years.

They are endangered.

endangered: close to dying out

21

READ MORE/WEBSITES

Clausen-Grace, Nicki. *Orangutans.* Wild Animal Kingdom. Mankato, MN: Black Rabbit Books, 2019.

Dickmann, Nancy. *Orangutans.* Animals in Danger. Tucson, AZ: Brown Bear Books, 2019.

Schuh, Mari. *The Supersmart Orangutan.* Supersmart Animals. Minneapolis: Lerner Publications, 2019.

Orangutan
kids.nationalgeographic.com/animals/orangutan/#orangutan-swinging-rope.jpg

Orangutan
kids.sandiegozoo.org/animals/orangutan

Orangutans
www.dkfindout.com/us/animals-and-nature/primates/orangutans/

GLOSSARY

endangered (in-DAYN-jurd)—close to dying out

honey (HUHN-ee)—a thick, sweet substance made by bees

insect (IN-sekt)—a small animal that has six legs

rain forest (REYN FAWR-ist)—a tropical forest that gets a lot of rain and has tall trees

INDEX